For Exuberant Grown-Ups

EXTREMELY ★ HAPPY ★ HOLIDAYS

DEVIN C. B. McEWAN
Art by SANDRA BOYNTON

RUNNING PRESS
PHILADELPHIA

Extremely Ha

To Victor "Trader Vic" Bergeron,
who died the day I was born.
Goodness knows what he did to deserve being
reincarnated as a far worse bartender.

—D. C. B. M.

Published by Running Press, an imprint of Hachette Book Group, Inc.
1290 Avenue of the Americas, New York, NY 10104
The Running Press name and logo are trademarks of Hachette Book Group, Inc.
ISBN: 979-8-89414-075-9   Printed in Malaysia   PCF   10 9 8 7 6 5 4 3 2 1   First Edition: October, 2025

Ex Libris Inebriatus

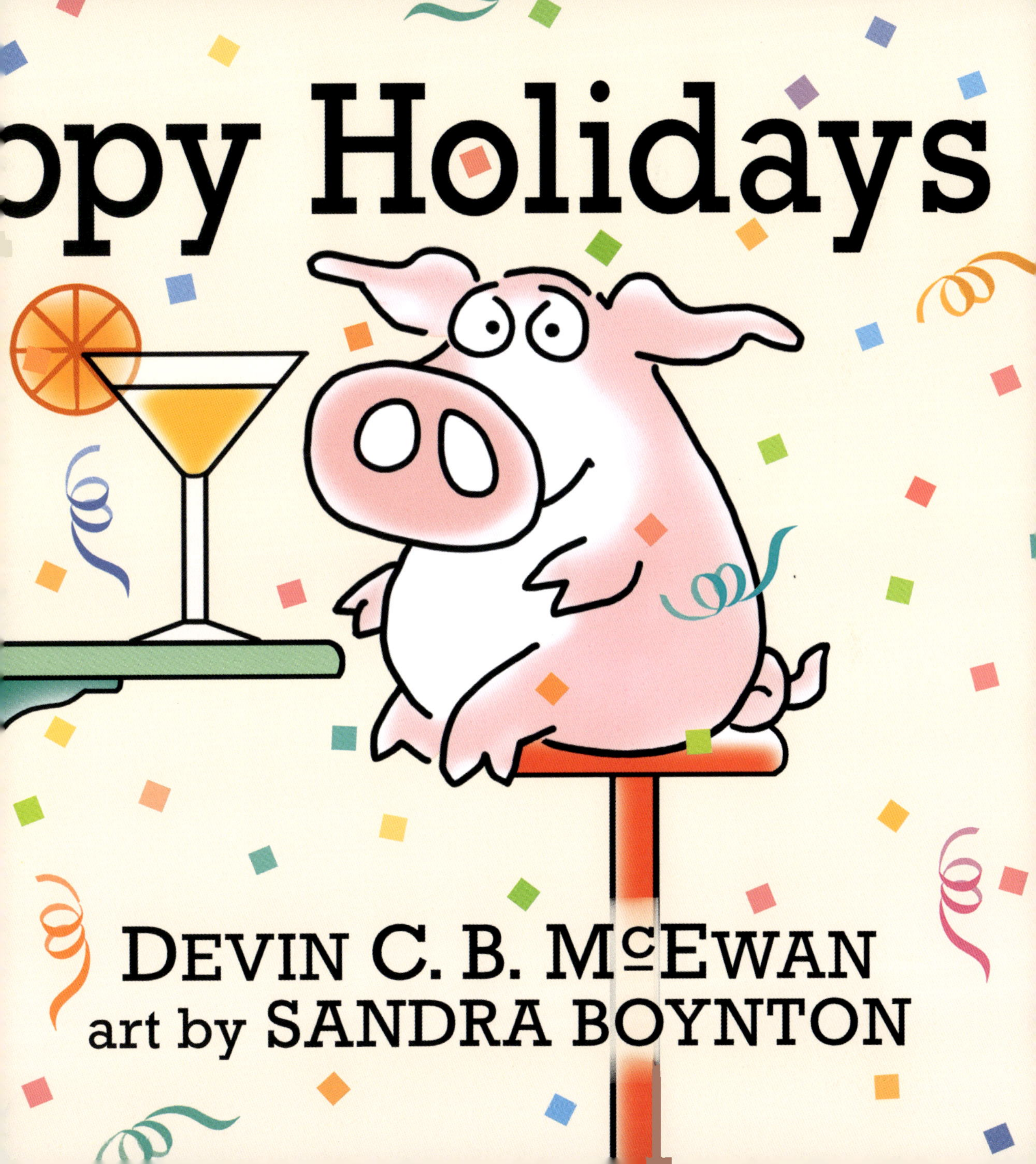
ppy Holidays
DEVIN C. B. McEWAN
art by SANDRA BOYNTON

Author's Confession

I am not, as will rapidly become apparent to the reader, a professional bartender.

This book came about like so: My best drinking buddy, who also happens to be my mother, who also happens to be cartoonist and children's book author Sandra Boynton, asked me to do a cocktail book with her, and I said yes.

It may or may not have been happy hour at the time.

Anyway, never one to let a lack of qualifications keep me from pursuing a goal, I threw together some drinks, set pen to paper (well, fingers to keyboard), and presto, a book!

Not necessarily a *good* book, mind you, but *a* book, no doubt about it.

I hope you enjoy reading it as much as I enjoyed writing it, but either way, hey, at least there are some really cute turkeys.

—Devin C. B. McEwan, BYOB

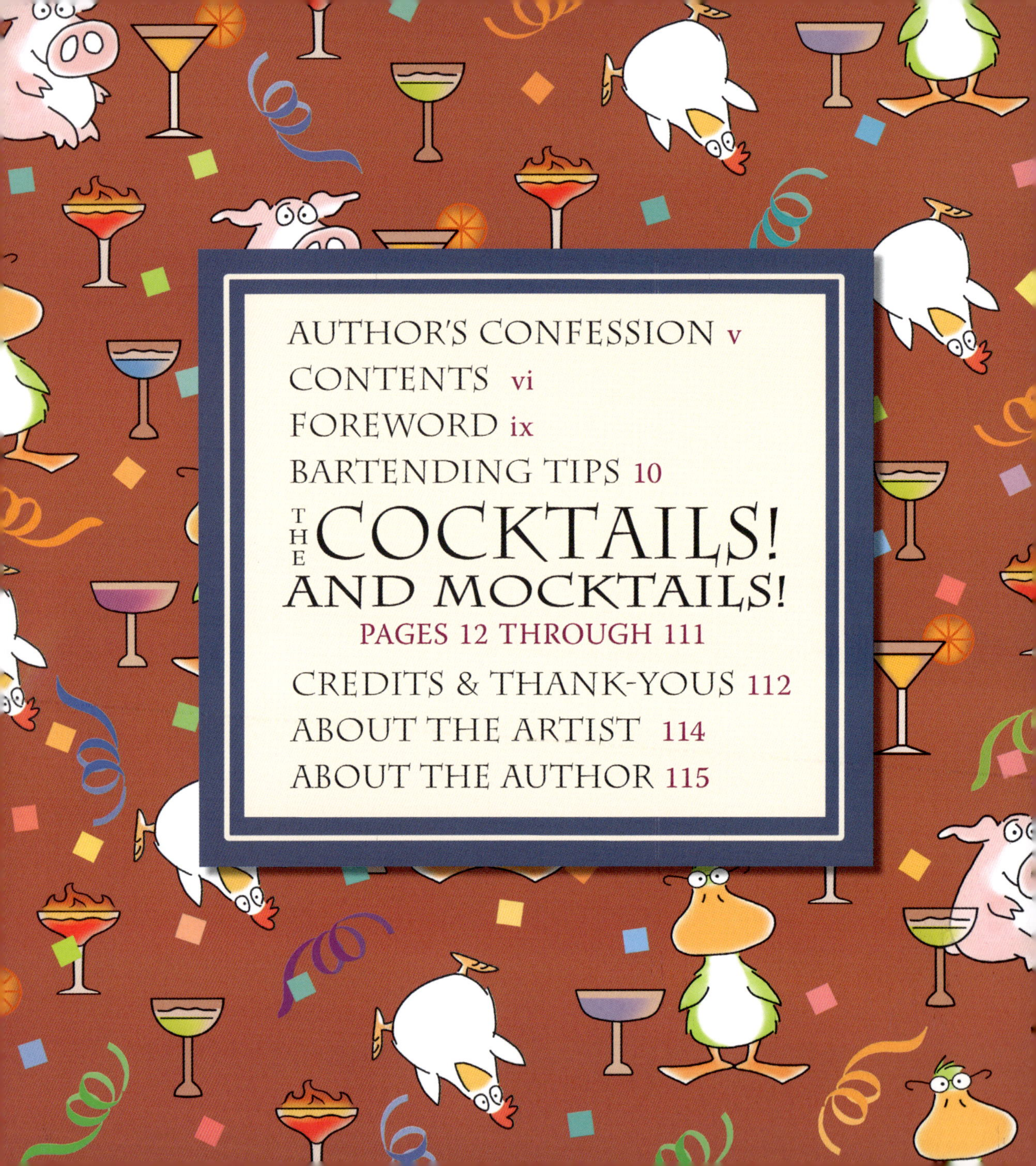

THE HOLIDAYS

FOREWORD

While the humble martini, old-fashioned, or jug of moonshine is a perfectly acceptable choice of drink most days of the year, at holiday time, something more festive is in order. Just as you wouldn't eat a hot dog for Thanksgiving dinner or watch professional badminton on Super Bowl Sunday or get your weather predictions from a human on Groundhog Day, nor should you be drinking anything ordinary on these or any other holiday. In the following pages, you'll find celebratory drinks for most major holidays, as well as one or two conspicuously non-major ones.

It should be noted that, as these drinks are intended for special occasions, many of them are more elaborate to make than your run-of-the-mill cocktail, involving techniques that might be unfamiliar to the casual home bartender. But fear not, gentle reader! These techniques will be explained in detail, and your extra efforts will be rewarded with the respect and admiration of your family and friends and, more importantly, the seething envy of your enemies.

BARTENDING TIPS

A WORD ON MEASURING

There are different philosophies when it comes to measuring cocktail ingredients. Your humble author is a real stickler for measuring; your humble illustrator is decidedly not. While I recommend precise measuring (using a jigger that can measure in ¼-oz increments), do whatever makes you happy—we already have your money.

A WORD ON JUICE

It might seem like an unnecessary extravagance to fresh-squeeze your own citrus juice when making cocktails—and objectively it *is*, in the same way that it's extravagant to thaw a frozen burrito before eating it. If you're someone who enjoys pleasure, however, trust me when I say you should juice your citrus right before using it and avoid like the plague the stuff that comes in a squeeze bottle.

RIMMING A GLASS Pour a small quantity of whatever you'll be rimming with onto a plate. Run a citrus wedge (or the inside of the spent shell from citrus you just juiced) around the rim of your glass and then dip the rim into the rimming ingredient.

SALINE SOLUTION

The secret weapon in the cocktail nerd's arsenal. Add a couple drops to your drinks; you won't taste the salt but you will taste the difference. To make, add 20 g fine, non-iodized salt to 80 g water in a dropper bottle and shake to combine.

It's important to label your saline solution properly.

EQUIPMENT

Listed below is all the stuff necessary to make every drink in this book as meticulously as possible. However, if you don't feel like shelling out for a bunch of specialized barware, feel free to channel your inner MacGyver and make do with common household items:

RECOMMENDED	POSSIBLE SUBSTITUTION
Bar spoon	Regular spoon duct-taped to butter knife
Cocktail shaker	Piggy bank
Fine-mesh strainer	Screen door
Jigger	Reckless abandon
Citrus juicer	Brute strength
Blender	Cement mixer
Paring knife	Sword stolen from mouse adventurer
Kitchen scale (that measures in grams)	Bathroom scale stolen from regular mouse
Mortar & pestle	Pestle & mortar
Nutmeg grater	Cheese grater (Do **not** substitute cheese for nutmeg!)
Grapefruit spoon	Regular spoon that accidentally fell in the garbage disposal
Plastic deli containers	Solid-gold deli containers
Coffee filters	Sock (clean)

GLASSWARE

INTO THE FUTURE!
INTO THE FUTURE!
INTO THE FUTURE!

January 1st

NEW YEAR'S DAY

WELCOME TO THE FUTURE!

It's been a slightly longer wait than advertised, but surely ***this*** will be the year that we finally get flying cars and teleporters and hand dryers that actually dry your hands.

The most hotly-anticipated innovation of all, however, is commercial space travel. To prepare our palates for the gustatory delights that await us on our journey among the stars, here's a space-age cocktail made with Tang and astronaut ice cream.

ASTRONAUT MIMOSA

built, coupe

YOU'LL NEED:

- 4 oz dry champagne
- 2 oz Tang*, chilled
- Neapolitan freeze-dried astronaut ice cream

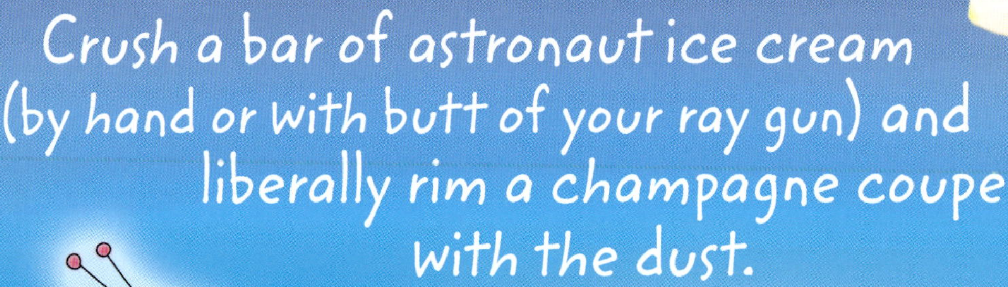

Crush a bar of astronaut ice cream (by hand or with butt of your ray gun) and liberally rim a champagne coupe with the dust.

Fill coupe with champagne and add Tang, stirring gently to combine.

*mix according to directions on package

★MOCKTAIL★

SPACE CAMP

built, coupe

YOU'LL NEED:

- 4 oz dry non-alcoholic sparkling wine
- 2 oz Tang*, chilled
- Neapolitan freeze-dried astronaut ice cream

Crush a bar of astronaut ice cream (by hand or with moon rock) and liberally rim a champagne coupe with the dust.

Fill coupe with sparkling wine and add Tang, stirring gently to combine.

*mix according to directions on package

February 2nd

GROUNDHOG DAY

Capricious
weather deities
are a common feature
of human civilizations
throughout the ages:
ZEUS
in Ancient Greece,
THOR
to the Vikings,

and, here in America,

PUNXSUTAWNEY PHIL.

Every February, we find ourselves at the mercy of this diminutive demigod. Will he see his shadow or won't he? Will it be six more weeks of winter or an early spring?

We must hope for the best but prepare for the worst, so here's a light, celebratory cocktail for if Phil doesn't see his shadow, and a warm, comforting one for if he does.

DO YOU FEEL LUCKY, PUNXSY?

shaken, coupe

SERVES 2!

4 oz kirsch
1 1/2 oz fresh lemon juice
1 1/2 oz honey syrup
8 g fresh mint leaves
4 drops saline solution

Combine kirsch, lemon juice, and mint in a blender and blend on high for a few seconds.

Strain through a fine-mesh strainer into a shaker and add honey syrup and saline solution.

Shake with ice and strain into chilled champagne coupes.

SHADOW OF THE GROUNDHOG

built, mug

SERVES 1!

1 1/2 oz Poire Williams
3 oz espresso, piping hot
3/4 oz demerara syrup
Lemon wheel

In a mug, add Poire Williams and demerara syrup to espresso and stir to combine. Float lemon wheel on top to garnish.

DEMERARA SYRUP

Add 200 g demerara sugar to 100 g water in a saucepan and bring to a simmer, stirring to dissolve sugar.

A GLASS TO PHIL

★MOCKTAIL★

shaken, coupe

SERVES 2!

2 oz unsweetened tart cherry juice
2 oz fresh lemon juice
2 oz honey syrup
8 g fresh mint leaves
4 drops saline solution

Combine ingredients in a blender and blend on high for a few seconds. Strain through a fine-mesh strainer into a shaker, shake with ice, and strain again into chilled champagne coupes.

HONEY SYRUP

Add 64 g hot water to 100 g clover honey and stir to combine. Let cool before using.

GRIN AND PEAR IT

★MOCKTAIL★

built, mug

SERVES 1!

4 oz espresso, piping hot
1 oz pear demerara syrup
Lemon wheel

In a mug, add pear demerara syrup to espresso and stir to combine. Float lemon wheel on surface to garnish.

PEAR DEMERARA SYRUP

Combine 200 g demerara sugar and 100 g water in a saucepan and bring to a simmer, stirring to dissolve sugar. Add a finely-cubed bosc pear and simmer for an additional 15 minutes, stirring occasionally. Strain and bottle.

(Pro tip: Keep those leftover pear cubes—they're AMAZING on vanilla ice cream.)

OWLS

10 20 30 40

10 20 30 40

2nd Sunday in February

SUPER BOWL SUNDAY

Superb Owl

When it comes to the Super Bowl, every second counts. For the players on the field, sure, I guess, but more importantly, for you, the viewer at home—one poorly-timed trip to the kitchen for a cold one or a snack and you risk missing the most crucial play of the game (or a really top-notch fabric softener commercial).

The solution?

Satisfy your beer and wings cravings in one fell swoop with this

Buffalo Wing Michelada.

BUFFALO WING MICHELADA

built, pint glass

YOU'LL NEED >>>>>

12 oz Mexican lager
1 oz lime juice, freshly squeezed
1 oz Frank's RedHot Original
Uncle Dan's Bleu Cheese powder

Rim a pint glass with the bleu cheese powder and fill with ice.

Pour beer into glass and add lime juice and hot sauce, stirring briefly to combine.

★MOCKTAIL★

ZERO YARD LINE

built, pint glass

12 oz non-alcoholic lager
1 oz lime juice, freshly squeezed
1 oz Frank's RedHot Original
Uncle Dan's Bleu Cheese powder

YOU'LL NEED <<<<<<

Rim a pint glass with the bleu cheese powder and fill with ice.

Pour beer into glass and add lime juice and hot sauce, stirring briefly to combine.

February 14th

VALENTINE'S DAY

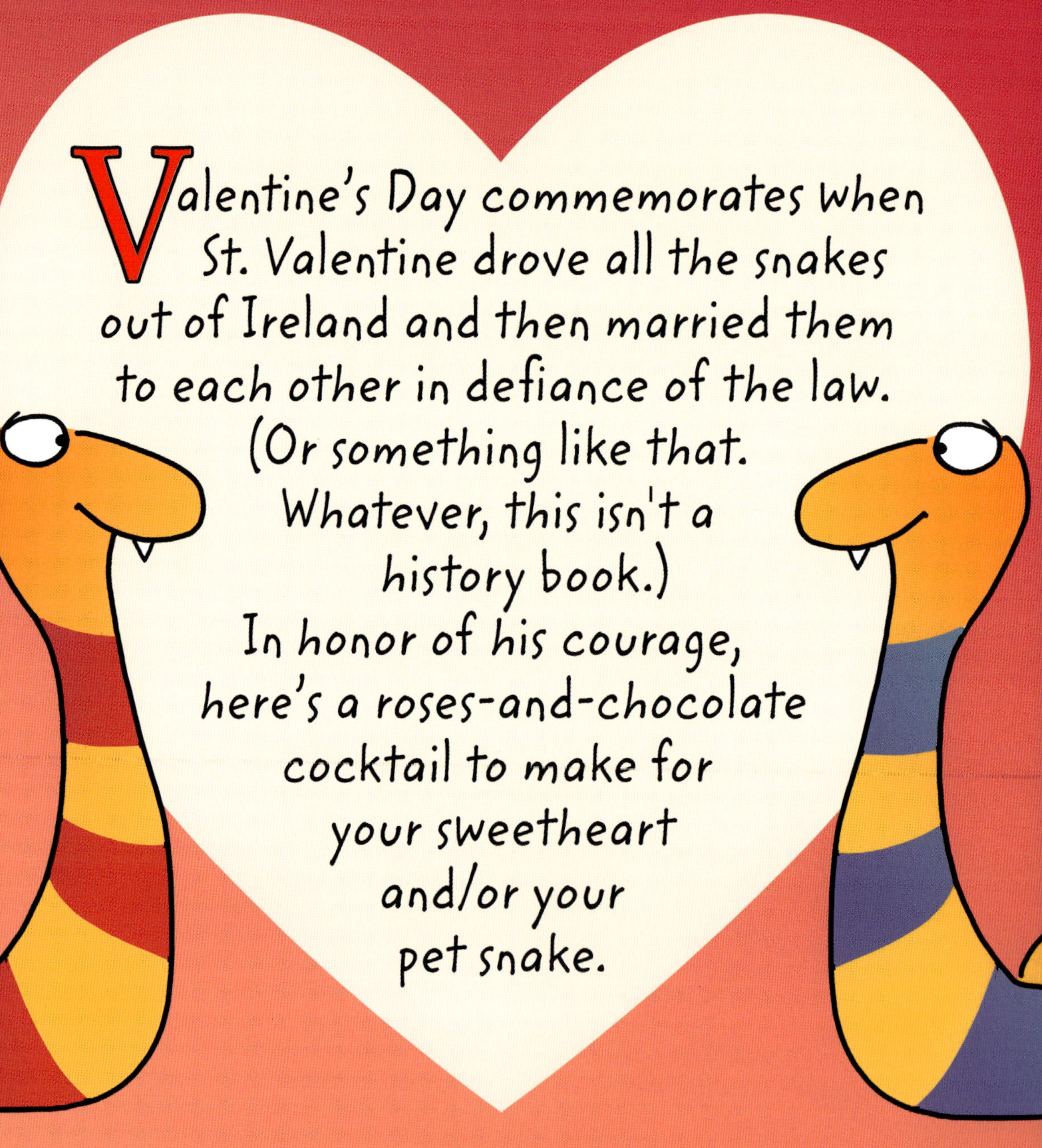

Valentine's Day commemorates when St. Valentine drove all the snakes out of Ireland and then married them to each other in defiance of the law. (Or something like that. Whatever, this isn't a history book.) In honor of his courage, here's a roses-and-chocolate cocktail to make for your sweetheart and/or your pet snake.

MAIN SQUEEZE

shaken, coupe

YOU'LL NEED:

- 2 oz gin
- 1 oz white crème de cacao
- 2 oz lemon juice, freshly squeezed
- 1 oz rose cordial [SEE NEXT PAGE]
- 4 drops saline solution [SEE P. 10]
- Rose petals

Shake with ice and strain into two chilled champagne coupes.

Float rose petals on surface to garnish.

SPECIAL TECHNIQUE

ROSE CORDIAL

Combine 200 g sugar and 200 g water in a saucepan and bring to a simmer, stirring to dissolve sugar.

Add a packed cup of dried rose petals, stir to combine, and simmer for 2 minutes.

Remove from heat, cover, and refrigerate for at least 24 hours before straining and bottling.

SERVES 2!

★MOCKTAIL★

HUGS & HISSES

shaken, coupe

YOU'LL NEED:

- 4 oz lemon juice, freshly squeezed
- 1 oz Torani crème de cacao syrup
- 1 oz rose cordial [SEE FACING PAGE]
- 4 drops saline solution [SEE P. 10]
- Rose petals

Shake with ice and strain into two chilled champagne coupes. Float rose petals on surface to garnish.

March 17th

ST. PATRICK'S DAY

Clan O'Potamus

When we think of St. Patrick's Day, one place springs inevitably to mind: Philadelphia.

Here, every March, local confectioners produce thousands of pounds of Irish Potato Candy — balls of coconut cream rolled in powdered cinnamon, resembling tiny potatoes.

Hippolyta O'Potamus
MT. AIRY CANDY SHOP

While the traditional cocktail of the holiday is, of course, six pints of Guinness back-to-back, for those looking to avoid gluten, excess calories, or bar fights, I've here adapted Irish Potato Candy into drink form.

SPUD TRANSFUSION

shaken, coupe

YOU'LL NEED:

- 2 oz Irish whiskey
- 1/2 oz Coco Lopez
- 1/2 oz heavy cream
- 1/4 oz cinnamon syrup (see below)
- Ground cinnamon

Shake with ice and strain into a chilled champagne coupe.

Dust with cinnamon.

Irish ewe a Happy St. Patrick's Day

CINNAMON SYRUP

With a mortar & pestle, mercilessly crush 3 cinnamon sticks.

Combine with 200 g sugar and 200 g water in a saucepan. Bring to a simmer, stirring to dissolve sugar.

Simmer for 2 minutes. Remove from heat and let cool before straining and bottling.

★MOCKTAIL★

MOCKTATO

shaken, coupe

YOU'LL NEED:

- 2 oz coconut water*
- 1/2 oz Coco Lopez
- 1/2 oz heavy cream
- 1/4 oz cinnamon syrup (see facing page)
- Ground cinnamon

Shake with ice and strain into a chilled champagne coupe.

Dust with cinnamon.

*While commercial coconut water will work perfectly well in this drink, water drained straight from a fresh coconut is ideal.

April 1st

DEFINITELY NOT APRIL FOOLS' DAY

In the course of researching this book, I happened upon the recipe for the original Shrimp Cocktail from V. Edwinn McCabe's 1873 bartending manual *The Libationist's Handbook*. This forgotten classic cocktail is a far cry from the appetizer shrimp "cocktail" popularized during Prohibition and still common today.

57. The Shrimp Cocktail

(Use large bar glass.)

1 jigger of Old Tom gin.

1 gill of tomato water
(See appendix p. 174.)

1 teaspoon-ful of prepared horseradish.

Fill tumbler with cooked shrimp, frozen solid.

Shake well and strain in a martini glass.

Ornament with a wedge of lemon.

APPENDIX 174

TOMATO WATER

Chop 1 lb. tomatoes and lightly salt.

Place the tomatoes in a jelly-bag over a bowl and set in the icehouse overnight to collect the nectareous liquid.

NOTE:
A jigger here means 2 oz, a gill 4 oz.

Shrimp Cocktail
circa 1873

(ARTIST'S RENDERING)

APRIL FOOL

Actually, no joke, it's a pretty good cocktail.

March/April (date varies)

EASTER

Hippoty hippoty hippoty hop.

In a remote corner of the Pacific Ocean lies Easter Island, a place shrouded in mystery. Who built the island's majestic moai? How did they accomplish such a feat? Where did all these bunnies come from? How do they subsist entirely on jelly beans? Did the author do any real research at all?

We may never know the answers.

(Have a drink.)

EASTER ISLAND

shaken, tall glass

YOU'LL NEED:

2 oz dark Jamaican rum
1 oz gold Virgin Islands rum
2 oz carrot juice
1 oz freshly-squeezed lime juice
1 oz falernum
2 dashes Angostura bitters
2 oz ginger beer, chilled
2 pineapple leaves
Jelly beans

Shake all ingredients (except ginger beer) with ice.
Strain into a tall glass filled with pebble ice.
Top with ginger beer and stir.
Garnish with pineapple-leaf bunny ears and a cocktail-umbrella skewer of jelly beans.

★MOCKTAIL★

VIRGIN ISLAND

shaken, tall glass

YOU'LL NEED:

3 oz carrot juice
1 1/2 oz freshly-squeezed lime juice
1 1/2 oz non-alcoholic falernum
3 oz ginger beer, chilled
2 pineapple leaves
Jelly beans

Shake all ingredients (except ginger beer) with ice. Strain into a tall glass filled with pebble ice. Top with ginger beer and stir. Garnish with pineapple-leaf bunny ears and jelly beans skewered on a cocktail umbrella.

May 5th

CINCO DE MAYO

Hippiñatamus

"Cinco de Mayo is a minor holiday in Mexico whose significance has been wildly exaggerated in the United States,"

Debbie Downers love to tell you—seemingly unaware that Americans need only the thinnest of pretexts for stuffing ourselves absolutely silly with tacos and inhaling pitchers of margaritas. The margarita is, in fact, the most popular cocktail in the U. S., which sets quite a high bar for anyone audacious enough to try and devise an original Cinco de Mayo cocktail. But **NO GUTS, NO GLORY**, right? Swing for the fences! Shoot for the moon!

Just kidding, I give up. Here's how to make a really good margarita:

THE QUITTER'S MARGARITA

shaken, margarita glass

NECESITARÁS:

2 oz jalapeño-infused Corazon blanco tequila*
3/4 oz Cointreau
3/4 oz fresh-squeezed lime juice
1/4 oz simple syrup [SEE NEXT PAGE]
5 drops saline solution [SEE P. 10]
Coarse sea salt

Burrito

Shake with ice and strain into an ice-filled margarita glass rimmed with sea salt.

* You can skip the jalapeño infusion if you wanna be a tiny little baby about it.

SPECIAL TECHNIQUES

JALAPEÑO-INFUSED CORAZON BLANCO TEQUILA

Thinly slice 3 jalapeños and combine in a jar with one 750 mL bottle of Corazon blanco tequila. Seal jar and shake vigorously.

Taste at intervals until desired heat level is reached, then strain through a fine-mesh strainer and funnel back into the tequila bottle.

Label the bottle, unless you're looking to prank your spice-intolerant friends.*

SIMPLE SYRUP

Put 200 g sugar and 200 g water in a blender and blend to combine.

JALAPEÑO SIMPLE SYRUP

Combine 200 g sugar and 200 g water in a saucepan and bring to a simmer, stirring to dissolve sugar. Add a thinly-sliced jalapeño, stir, and simmer for 10 minutes. Remove from heat and let cool before straining and bottling.

---

* Millicent and Eugene.

★MOCKTAIL★

JALAPEÑO BUSINESS

shaken, margarita glass

NECESITARÁS:

1 oz pineapple juice
1 oz fresh-squeezed lime juice
1 oz jalapeño simple syrup [SEE FACING PAGE]
5 drops saline solution [SEE P. 10]
Tajin

Shake with ice and strain into an ice-filled margarita glass rimmed with Tajin.

2nd Sunday in May

MOTHER'S DAY

OOPS!

You meant to bring Mom breakfast in bed for the holiday but it took you a *little* bit longer than expected to start your day and now it's 5 p.m.

No problemo!
This cocktail offers all of her breakfast favorites in one convenient, drinkable package.

BREAKFAST IN BED №1

shaken, coupe

YOU'LL NEED:

- 2 oz sausage-washed bourbon [SEE P. 71]
- 3/4 oz lemon-acid grapefruit juice [SEE P. 64]
- 3/4 oz Earl Grey honey syrup [SEE P. 64]
- 2 drops saline solution [SEE PAGE 10]
- 1 oz egg white
- Mini-pancake stack [SEE P. 65]

Dry shake (shake without ice) for about 10 seconds.

Add ice, shake, and strain into a champagne coupe.

Garnish with mini-pancake stack skewered on a cocktail pick.

SPECIAL TECHNIQUES

LEMON-ACID GRAPEFRUIT JUICE

To 100 mL fresh-squeezed grapefruit juice, add 4 g citric acid and stir to combine.

EARL GREY HONEY SYRUP

Steep an Earl Grey tea bag in 6 oz boiling water for 5 minutes. Remove tea bag, immediately add 64 g of the tea to 100 g clover honey, and stir to combine. Let cool before using.

Tea Rex "Earl of the Dinosaurs"

THE TEA-TOTALER

★MOCKTAIL★

shaken, coupe

YOU'LL NEED:

2 oz lemon-acid grapefruit juice [SEE FACING PAGE]
1 oz Earl Grey honey syrup [SEE FACING PAGE]
2 drops saline solution [SEE PAGE 10]
1 oz egg white
Mini-pancake stack [SEE BELOW]

Dry shake (shake without ice) for about 10 seconds. Add ice, shake, and strain into a chilled champagne coupe. Garnish with mini-pancake stack skewered on a cocktail pick.

MINI-PANCAKE STACK

adapted from Andrew Rea's superb pancake recipe

- 1¾ oz (by weight) all-purpose flour
- 1½ tsp sugar
- ½ tsp baking powder
- ¼ tsp salt
- ⅛ tsp baking soda
- ½ cup buttermilk
- 1 quail egg
- 2 tsp melted butter, cooled

In a medium bowl, whisk together dry ingredients. In a separate bowl, whisk together wet ingredients. Add wet ingredients to dry and whisk until just combined (batter should still be lumpy). Cover batter and let rest in fridge for at least 30 minutes. Pour quarter-sized blobs of batter into an unoiled skillet over medium heat and cook until bottom edge of pancake starts to curl under; flip and cook until bottom is golden brown.

3rd Sunday in June

FATHER'S DAY

Dad would like his breakfast in cocktail form, too, but, y'know, **MANLY.**

(But still in a cute little coupe with a cute little garnish, please.)

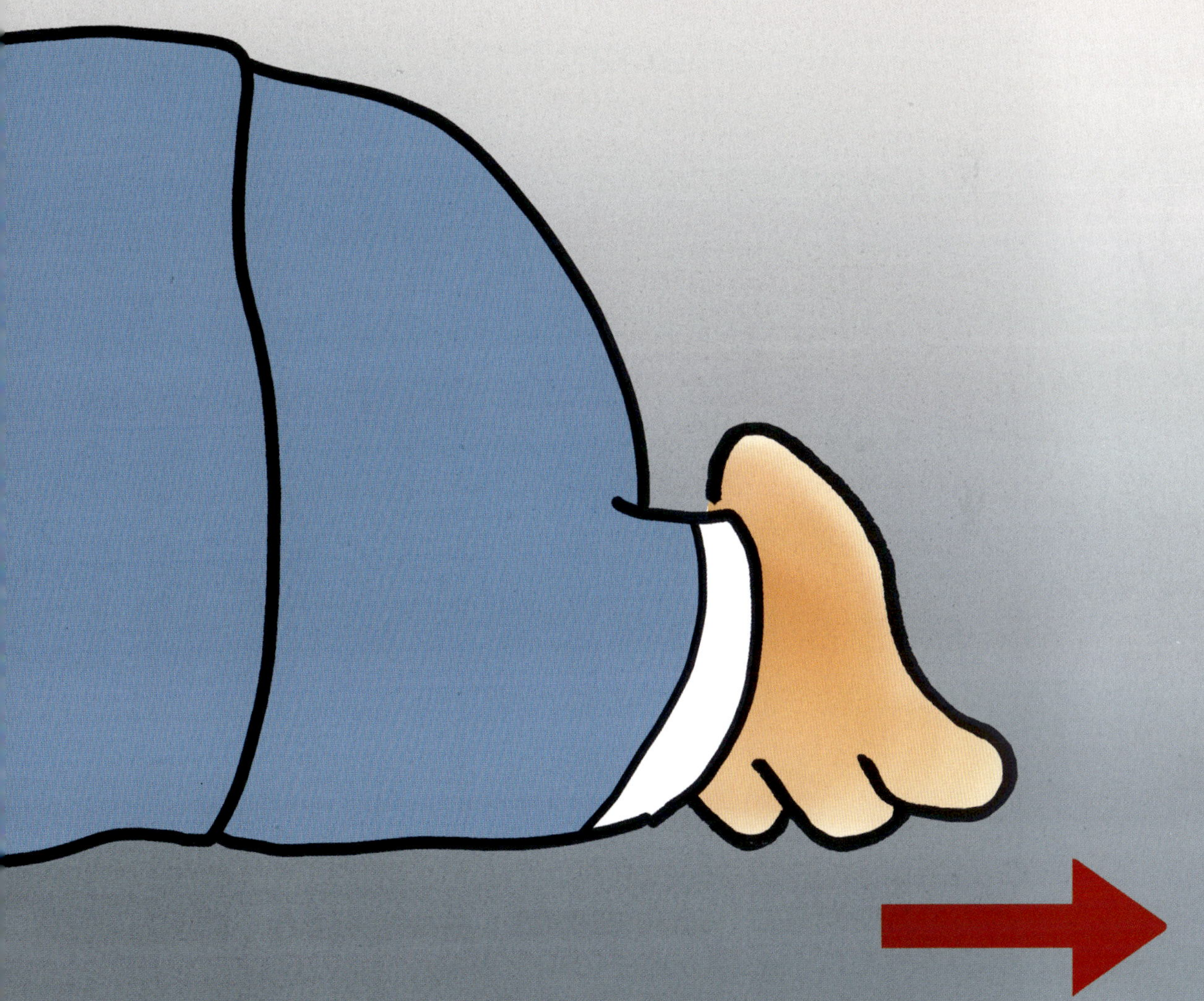

BREAKFAST IN BED №2

shaken, coupe

YOU'LL NEED:

2 oz bacon-washed bourbon [SEE FACING PAGE]
3/4 oz lemon-acid orange juice [SEE P. 74]
1/2 oz maple syrup
1/4 oz coffee brandy
2 drops saline solution [SEE P. 10]
1 oz egg white
Mini stroopwafel (available wherever fine stroopwafels are sold)

Grin and bear

Dry shake (shake without ice) for about 10 seconds. Add ice, shake, and strain into a champagne coupe. Garnish with mini stroopwafel.

MOCKTAIL

shaken, coupe

A COUPE OF JOE

YOU'LL NEED:

2 oz lemon-acid orange juice [SEE P. 74]
3/4 oz coffee syrup (I use Autocrat brand)
2 drops saline solution [SEE P. 10]
1 oz egg white
Mini stroopwafel (available wherever fine stroopwafels are sold)

Dry shake (shake without ice) for about 10 seconds. Add ice, shake, and strain into a chilled champagne coupe. Garnish with mini stroopwafel.

SPECIAL TECHNIQUE

BACON-WASHED/SAUSAGE-WASHED BOURBON

Cook a package of bacon or ground breakfast sausage and reserve the fat. Add 60 g liquid bacon/sausage fat to 750 ml bourbon in a wide-mouth container (like a large mason jar) and shake vigorously to combine. Let rest 1 hour, shaking occasionally for the first half hour. Place in freezer for several hours until the fat forms a solid puck at the top. With a skewer or other pokey implement, poke two holes in the puck—one for pouring and one for air. Strain the mixture through a coffee filter. (Use additional filters if the first one clogs.)

4th of July

INDEPENDENCE DAY

SPECIAL TECHNIQUES

SUGARED TANQUERAY GIN

Add 160 g superfine sugar to 750 mL Tanqueray gin in a sealed container and shake like crazy until sugar is completely dissolved.

LEMON-ACID ORANGE JUICE

To 100 mL fresh-squeezed orange juice, add 5 g citric acid and stir to combine.

ORGEAT

While you *can* make your own orgeat, it's a bit of an ordeal, so I recommend using a commercial brand if available. (If not, *artofdrink.com* has a good recipe.)

SIMPLE SYRUP

Put 200 g sugar and 200 g water into a blender and blend to combine.

What could be a more reverent, solemn, and noble way to celebrate America and her cultural melting pot than taking three cherished cocktails from around the world (the negroni, the margarita, and the Mai Tai), making slushies out of them, and layering them to look like a Bomb Pop?

SERVES 6!

THE MELTING POP

frozen, pilsner glass

★ RED LAYER (frozen negroni)

MIX IN ITS OWN DELI CONTAINER WITH LID—SHAKE TO COMBINE:

2 1/2 oz sugared Tanqueray gin [SEE P. 74]
1 oz Campari
1 oz vermouth bianco
1 oz lemon-acid orange juice [SEE P. 74]
8 drops saline solution [SEE P. 10]
4 oz water

★ WHITE LAYER (frozen margarita)

MIX IN ITS OWN DELI CONTAINER WITH LID—SHAKE TO COMBINE:

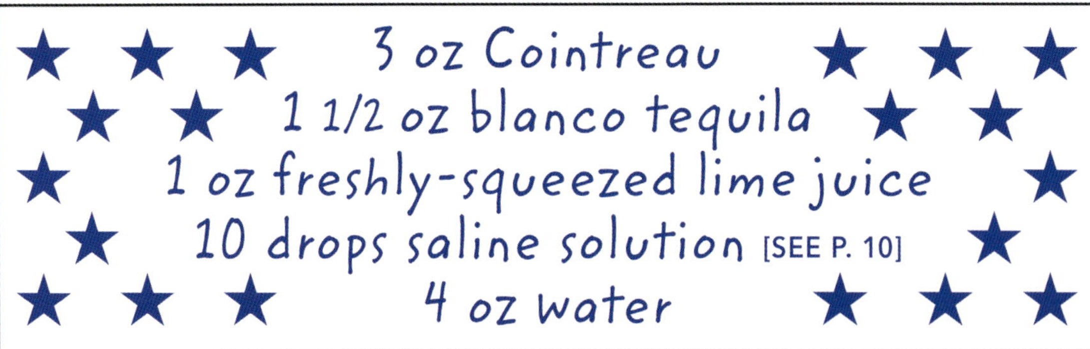

3 oz Cointreau
1 1/2 oz blanco tequila
1 oz freshly-squeezed lime juice
10 drops saline solution [SEE P. 10]
4 oz water

BLUE LAYER (frozen Mai Tai)

MIX IN ITS OWN DELI CONTAINER WITH LID—SHAKE TO COMBINE:

2 1/2 oz Wray & Nephew white rum
1 oz blue curaçao
1 oz freshly-squeezed lime juice
1/2 oz orgeat [SEE P. 74]
1/2 oz simple syrup [SEE P. 74]
8 drops saline solution [SEE P. 10]
4 oz water

Freeze the three containers overnight.

At serving time, give each of the three mixtures a stir and then layer with a spoon into a pilsner glass.

Garnish with a sparkler.

YO HO HO, ME
HEARTIES! AHOY
AVAST YE! AYE
GIVE IT THE OLD
HEAVE-HO
SCUPPER THAT
SHIVER ME TIMBERS
LOOK LIVELY
SAVVY, MATEY
ARRR! BLIMEY

September 19th be

TALK LIKE A PIRATE DAY

~~Avast ye, scurvy dogs!~~ Salutations, friends!

~~Shiver me timbers,~~ Why, bless my soul,

~~be~~ is that a sea monster on the horizon? ~~Nay, 'tis but~~ No,, it is only the Calamartini, a most ~~bracing grog~~ fortifying beverage for ~~salts~~ sailors and ~~landlubbers~~ non-sailors alike.

~~Drink up, me hearties!~~ Enjoy!

THE CALAMARTINI

shaken, martini glass

YOU'LL NEED:

3 oz navy-strength gin
1 oz dry vermouth
1 bar spoon (1/8 oz) squid ink
Squid tentacle
(or octopus will do if you're fresh out of squid)

Shake* with ice and strain into a chilled martini glass.

Garnish with the tentacle. (Don't argue, just do it.)

*Much ink has been spilled over whether a martini should properly be shaken or stirred, but in this case shaking is necessary in order to incorporate the squid ink.

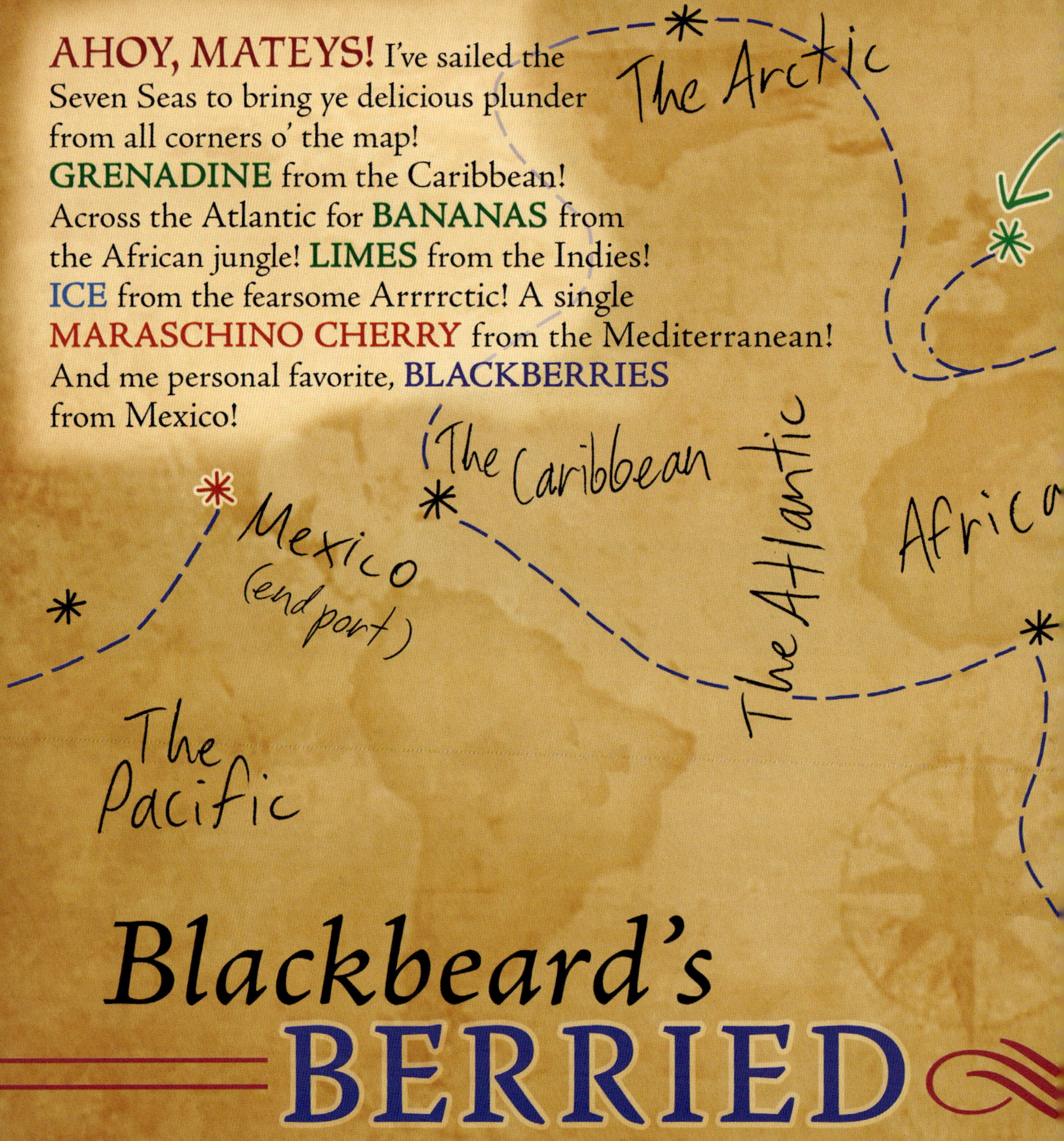

AHOY, MATEYS! I've sailed the Seven Seas to bring ye delicious plunder from all corners o' the map! **GRENADINE** from the Caribbean! Across the Atlantic for **BANANAS** from the African jungle! **LIMES** from the Indies! **ICE** from the fearsome Arrrrctic! A single **MARASCHINO CHERRY** from the Mediterranean! And me personal favorite, **BLACKBERRIES** from Mexico!

Blackbeard's BERRIED

London (port of origin)

The Mediterranean

★MOCKTAIL★

½ CUP BLACKBERRIES
½ BANANA
1 ½ OZ LIME JUICE, FRESHLY SQUEEZED
½ OZ GRENADINE
½ CUP ICE
MARASCHINO CHERRY
2 DROPS SALINE SOLUTION

PUT EVERYTHING (EXCEPTING THE CHERRY) IN A BLENDER & BLEND UNTIL SMOOTH. POUR INTO A TIKI MUG. GARNISH WITH THE CHERRY.

The Indies

Wait, that be only **SIX** seas.
Arrgh. What am I forgettin'?
Oh, right, the Pacific!
Er...**SALTWATER** from the Pacific!
(No rum, though—we drank it all en route.
YO HO HO!)

TREASURE

BOO!
EEK!

October 31st

HALLOWEEN

Being a grown-up is hard. Taxes, back pain, feigning interest in televised golf, and worst of all, no more trick-or-treating. (Unless you decide to have kids, which frankly is a pretty big commitment just to get some free candy.) Yes, Halloween isn't quite the same once you reach the age where threats of minor vandalism are no longer rewarded with miniature Snickers bars.

Still, adulthood does have its perks:

1. The ability to purchase rum

That's all I've got. But what more could you need? Don your spookiest ghost or witch or enterprise risk management actuary costume and whip up a **BOO-TIKI DRINK**, easily one of the top three orangest cocktails in this book.

TRICK or TREAT

BOO-TIKI DRINK

blended, tiki mug

YOU'LL NEED:

3/4 oz gold Puerto Rican rum
3/4 oz dark Jamaican rum
1/2 oz 151-proof Demerara rum
(plus 2 oz more for igniting jack-o'-lantern orange)
2 oz pumpkin pie mix
1 oz Coco Lopez
1 oz fresh-squeezed lime juice
1/2 oz candy corn syrup*
8 oz (1 cup) crushed ice
Jack-o'-lantern orange*

Put everything (except jack-o'-lantern orange) in a blender and blend until smooth. Pour into a a tiki mug. Rest jack-o'-lantern orange atop mouth of mug. Pour 2 oz 151-proof rum into the orange and ignite with a match. Trick AND treat!

*See next page

SPECIAL TECHNIQUES

CANDY CORN SYRUP

Combine 200 g candy corn and 200 g water in a saucepan and bring to a simmer, stirring until candy corn is completely dissolved. Let cool before using.

JACK-O'-LANTERN ORANGE

With a washable marker, draw a jack-o'-lantern face on an orange. Cut the top off the orange and scoop out the inside with a grapefruit spoon. With a paring knife (or an X-Acto knife if you've got one), cut out the face.

★MOCKTAIL★

NO BOOS

blended, tiki mug

YOU'LL NEED:

- 3 oz pumpkin pie mix
- 1 1/2 oz Coco Lopez
- 1 1/2 oz freshly-squeezed lime juice
- 1/2 oz candy corn syrup [SEE FACING PAGE]
- 8 oz (1 cup) crushed ice
- Jack-o'-lantern orange

Put everything (except jack-o'-lantern orange) in a blender and blend until smooth.

Pour into a tiki mug.

Rest jack-o'-lantern orange atop mouth of mug.

4th Thursday in November

THANKSGIVING

A mysterious stranger handed me this recipe and then vanished into the night.

Thank you, kind stranger!

WILD TURKEYS

[COULDN'T DRAG ME AWAY]

THIS IS THE ONLY TURKEY RECIPE YOU'LL NEED FOR A VERY HAPPY THANKSGIVING.

A FRIEND

2 oz butter-washed Wild Turkey 101 bourbon*
1/4 oz candied yam syrup*
2 dashes cranberry bitters
Orange twist
3 brandied cranberries*

Place ice cubes [or, better yet, a single 2" X 2" X 2" ice cube] in an old-fashioned glass.

Add, in order: bitters, bourbon, and syrup. Stir for 5 seconds.

Garnish with orange twist and brandied cranberries skewered on a cocktail pick.

*SEE OTHER SIDE

SPECIAL TECHNIQUES

BUTTER-WASHED WILD TURKEY

Melt 240 g butter, add to 750 mL Wild Turkey bourbon in a wide-mouth container (like a large mason jar), and shake vigorously to combine. Let rest 1 hour,shaking occasionally for the first half hour. Place in freezer for several hours until the butter forms a solid puck at the top. With a skewer or other pokey implement, poke two holes in the puck, one for pouring and one for air. Strain the bourbon through a coffee filter.(You may need to use additional filters if the first one clogs.)

CANDIED YAM SYRUP

Drain the liquid from a can of candied yams. Add equal parts (by weight) yam liquid and sugar to a blender and blend to combine.

BRANDIED CRANBERRIES

Combine 200 g sugar and 200 g water in a saucepan and bring to a simmer, stirring to dissolve sugar. Add 200 g cranberries and cook for 5 minutes. Remove from heat and let cool before adding 1 cup brandy, stirring to combine. Transfer cranberries and syrup to a mason jar, seal, and refrigerate for at least 24 hours before using.

PET TURKEY

★MOCKTAIL★

shaken, coupe

YOU'LL NEED:

- 3/4 oz cranberry juice
- 3/4 oz fresh-squeezed lime juice
- 3/4 oz fresh-squeezed orange juice
- 3/4 oz candied yam syrup [SEE FACING PAGE]
- 2 drops saline solution [SEE PAGE 10]
- Orange twist

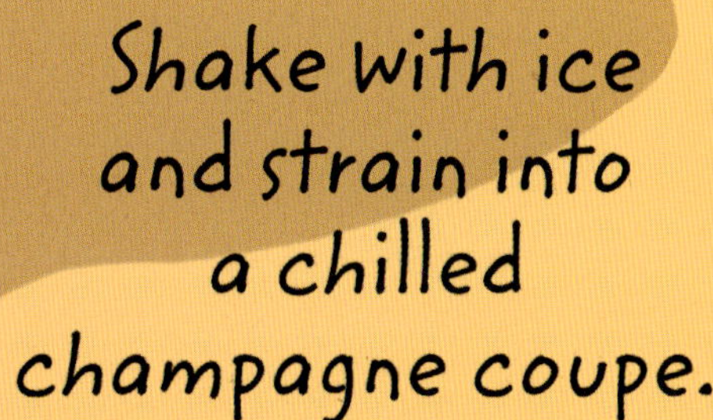

Shake with ice and strain into a chilled champagne coupe.

Garnish with orange twist.

November / December (date varies)

HANUKKAH

In honor of the miracle of the oil, it's traditional to eat fried foods for the eight days of Hanukkah—which, for Americans, really isn't that big an ask, since it's traditional for us to eat fried foods the other 357 days of the year as well.

The latke (a fried potato pancake) is the undisputed king of Hanukkah noshes and has only one conspicuous drawback: It isn't drinkable.

Until now!

LATKETINI

stirred, martini glass

YOU'LL NEED:

- 2 1/2 oz schmaltz-washed or olive oil-washed potato vodka [SEE NEXT PAGE]
- 1/2 oz dry vermouth
- Dash of Dashfire apple bitters
- Cocktail onions

Stir with ice and strain into a chilled martini glass.

Garnish with cocktail onions.

SPECIAL TECHNIQUES

SCHMALTZ-WASHED POTATO VODKA

Add 240 g liquid schmaltz to 750 mL potato vodka in a wide-mouth container (like a large mason jar) and shake vigorously to combine. Let rest 1 hour, shaking occasionally for the first half hour. Place in freezer for several hours until the schmaltz forms a solid puck at the top. With a skewer or other pokey implement, poke two holes in the puck—one for pouring and one for air. Strain the vodka through a coffee filter. (You may need to use additional filters if the first one clogs.)

OLIVE OIL-WASHED POTATO VODKA

Add 240 g extra-virgin olive oil to 750 mL potato vodka in a wide-mouth container (like a large mason jar) and shake vigorously to combine. Let rest 1 hour, shaking occasionally for the first half hour. Place in freezer for several hours until the olive oil forms a solid puck at the top. With a skewer or other pokey implement, poke two holes in the puck—one for pouring and one for air. Strain the vodka through a coffee filter. (You may need to use additional filters if the first one clogs.)

★MOCKTAIL★

THE GOLDEN EGG

whisked, coupe

YOU'LL NEED:

2 oz whole milk
30 g (about 5 coins) gelt, foil removed
3 1/2 oz club soda, chilled
Gold leaf

In a saucepan over low heat, bring milk to a simmer. Add gelt and stir until completely dissolved. Transfer to a container with a spout and refrigerate. Once chilled, slowly add club soda, whisking to a froth with a fork. Pour into a chilled champagne coupe. Garnish with gold leaf.

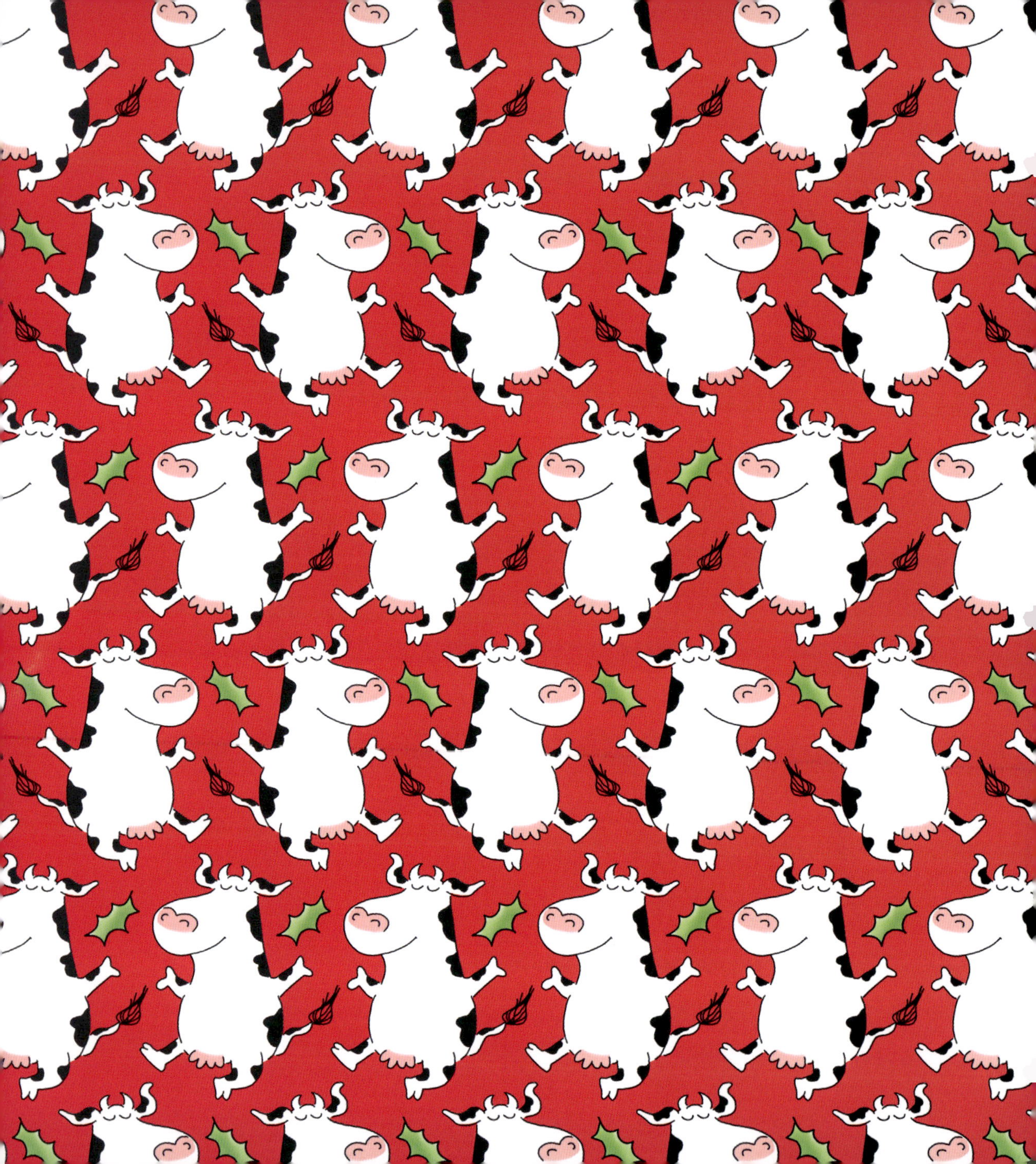

December 25th

CHRISTMAS

"Not a creature was stirring..."

So you're nestled in your chalet in Jalisco, trimming the Christmas agave. "Rudolfo el reno de la nariz roja" is wafting from the stereo.

What to serve with those goose quesadillas you've got cooking on the stove...

Why not a nice refreshing

Noggarita,

just like Abuela used to make?

SERVES 6!

¡EL NOGGARITA!

blended, margarita glass

YOU'LL NEED:

- 8 oz añejo tequila
- 3 oz Grand Marnier
- 6 large eggs
- 30 oz half and half
- 3 oz agave nectar
- Freshly-grated nutmeg

Beat eggs in a blender for 1 minute on medium speed.

Add tequila, Grand Marnier, half and half, and agave nectar and blend until combined.

Refrigerate overnight.

Serve in nutmeg-rimmed margarita glasses.

MOCKTAIL VERSION →

FELIZ
NOGGARITA
"¡PA' ARRIBA, PA' ABAJO..

★MOCKTAIL★

SERVES 6! (OR 15,684 MICE)

¡EL NOGGARITA MÓCTEL!

blended, margarita glass

YOU'LL NEED:

- 8 large eggs
- 40 oz half and half
- 3 oz agave nectar
- 1 oz Rose's lime juice*
- Freshly-grated nutmeg

*I know, I know, I told you to use only fresh-squeezed citrus juice—but in this instance we want lime flavor without curdling the half and half, so we must form an unholy alliance with our old archnemesis, Rose's lime juice.

Beat eggs in a blender for 1 minute on medium speed.

Add half and half, agave nectar, and Rose's lime juice and blend until combined.

Refrigerate overnight.

Serve in nutmeg-rimmed margarita glasses.

…PA' CENTRO, PA' DENTRO!"

December 31st

NEW YEAR'S EVE

Some year or another, you've probably found yourself at midnight on New Year's Eve, resplendent in your cardboard top hat, pondering a mystery that has baffled revelers for centuries:

"What the heck is an Auld Lang Syne?"

We have Robert Burns (1759-1796), Scotland's national poet, to thank for this inscrutable phrase, which, translated from Scots to English, means "Old Long Since", though that still isn't quite English, let's be honest.

In addition to his lasting contributions to nonsense lyrics, Burns lends his name to a classic cocktail, the Bobby Burns, to which this champagne drink is an *homage*.*

*French for "old long since".

BUBBLY BURNS

shaken, coupe

YOU'LL NEED:

1 1/2 oz scotch
1/2 oz sweet vermouth
1/2 oz lemon juice, freshly squeezed
1/2 oz simple syrup [SEE P. 58]
1 tsp Benedictine
2 oz dry champagne
Lemon twist

Shake all ingredients (except champagne) with ice. Strain into a champagne coupe. Add champagne, stirring gently to combine. Garnish with lemon twist.

At the stroke of midnight, head on back to page 12, NEW YEAR'S DAY.

CHE

This book wouldn't exist without the following people, but please don't hold that against them:

DAVE ARNOLD, whose book *Liquid Intelligence* taught me everything I've ever known about making cocktails, all of which I promptly forgot as soon as I started writing this book.

JEFF "BEACHBUM" BERRY, whose books are as wildly entertaining as they are instructive. I've spilled so many cocktail ingredients on my copy of *Beachbum Berry Remixed* that I could probably wring a Mai Tai out of it.

The fine folks at STATELINE WINE & SPIRITS in Canaan, Connecticut; DOMANEY'S LIQUORS & FINE WINES in Great Barrington, Massachusetts; and SALISBURY WINES in Salisbury, Connecticut—especially JIMMY KENNEDY, who special-ordered my every bizarre request without batting an eye. I bet I could've asked for unicorn tears and he would've found a way to make it happen.

TERRY ORTOLANI of Pint-Size Productions, a prince among printers and a swell guy to boot.

ERS!

Ryan Bailey for the dashing moai who preside over page 50. (Pictured here listening to—what else?—hard rock.)

Ashley Adkins, for letting me swipe the name "Astronaut Mimosa." You will not be receiving any royalties.

Shannon Fabricant and Kristin Kiser at Running Press, for their support and guidance and for cheerfully tolerating my very loose interpretation of the word "deadline."

My fearless guinea pigs:

Darcy Boynton, Keith Boynton, Ashleigh Rader, Kyle Boynton, Colleen Benedict, Brett Benzio, Ali DeProdocini, Evan Downey, Christine Gray, Westy Kiefer, Jordan Sherman, David Ruchman, Willie Clarke, Ricky Powell, and Laura Tabaka

(Sorry about that beta version of Breakfast in Bed № 2, you guys.)

—D. C. B. M.

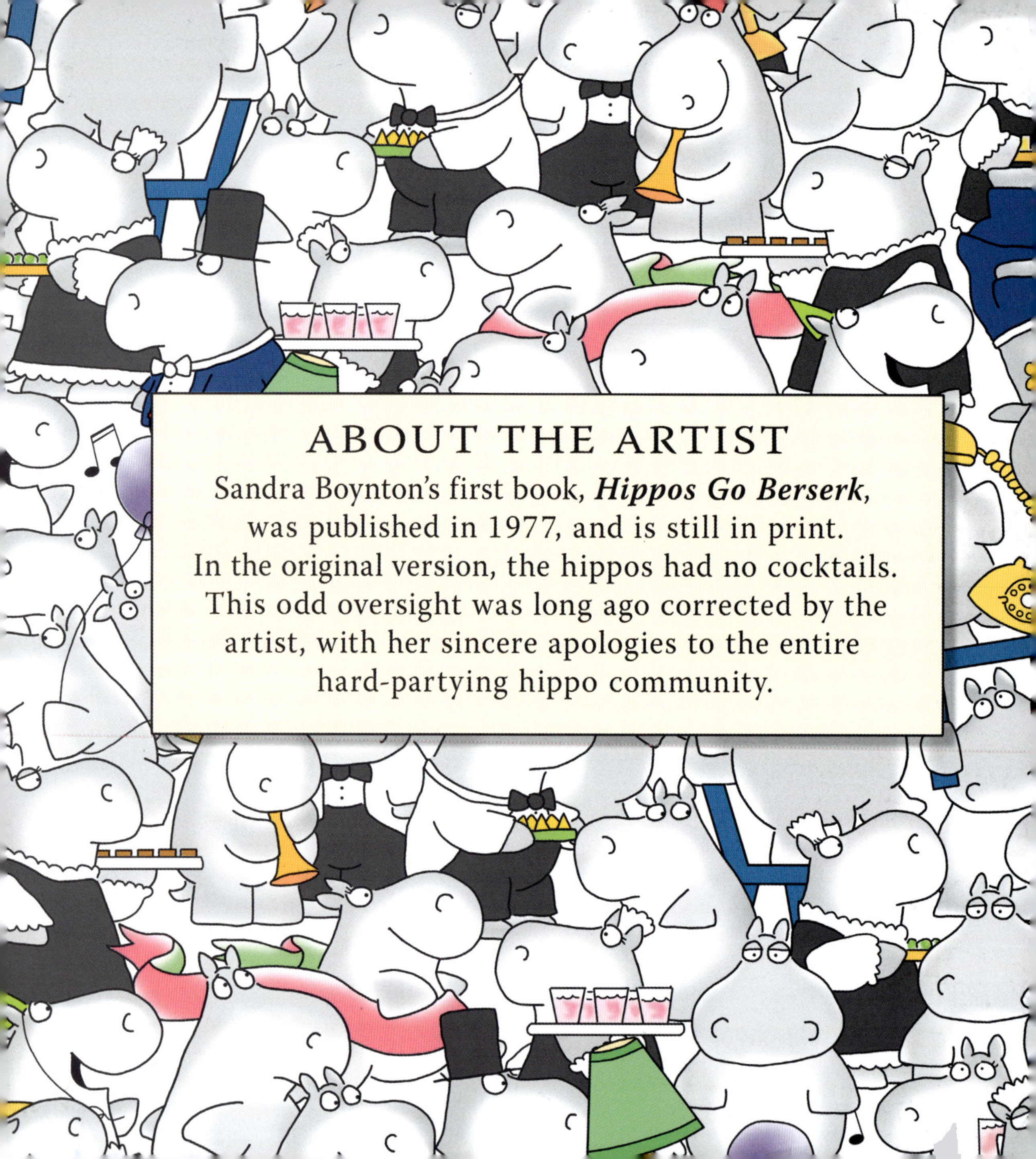

ABOUT THE ARTIST

Sandra Boynton's first book, ***Hippos Go Berserk***, was published in 1977, and is still in print. In the original version, the hippos had no cocktails. This odd oversight was long ago corrected by the artist, with her sincere apologies to the entire hard-partying hippo community.